D0282861

DRUG
DANGERS

LSD, PCP, and HALLUCINOGEN
DRUG DANGERS

Judy Monroe

Enslow Publishers, Inc.

40 Industrial Road   PO Box 38
Box 398   Aldershot
Berkeley Heights, NJ 07922   Hants GU12 6BP
USA   UK

http://www.enslow.com

Library of Congress Cataloging-in-Publication Data

Monroe, Judy.
    LSD, PCP, and hallucinogen drug dangers / Judy Monroe.
        p.   cm. – (Drug dangers)
    Includes bibliographical references and index.
    Summary: Examines the social, medical, and legal aspects of
hallucinogens and related drugs, the effects of their abuse, and
different treatment programs.
    ISBN 0-7660-1318-9
    1. Drug abuse—United States Juvenile literature. 2. Drug abuse—
United States—Prevention Juvenile literature. 3. Teenagers—Drug use
United States Juvenile literature. [1. Drug abuse.]
    I. Title II. Series
    HV5809.5.M66   2000
    362.29'4—dc21
                                                    99-14105
                                                        CIP

Printed in the United States of America

10 9 8 7 6 5 4 3 2 1

To Our Readers:
All Internet addresses in this book were active and appropriate when we
went to press. Any comments or suggestions can be sent by e-mail to
Comments@enslow.com or to the address on the back cover.

Photo Credits: Corel Corporation, pp. 9, 25, 37, 39, 42; Díamar Interactive
Corp., pp. 16, 47, 54; Drug Enforcement Administration, pp. 14, 20; Mary Ann
Littell, p. 12; National Archives, pp. 6, 28, 32

Cover Photo: © Corel Corporation.

contents

Titles in the **Drug Dangers** series:

Alcohol Drug Dangers
ISBN 0-7660-1159-3

Amphetamine Drug Dangers
ISBN 0-7660-1321-9

Crack and Cocaine Drug Dangers
ISBN 0-7660-1155-0

Diet Pill Drug Dangers
ISBN 0-7660-1158-5

Ecstasy and Other Designer Drug Dangers
ISBN 0-7660-1322-7

Herbal Drug Dangers
ISBN 0-7660-1319-7

Heroin Drug Dangers
ISBN 0-7660-1156-9

Inhalant Drug Dangers
ISBN 0-7660-1153-4

LSD, PCP, and Hallucinogen Drug Dangers
ISBN 0-7660-1318-9

Marijuana Drug Dangers
ISBN 0-7660-1214-X

Speed and Methamphetamine Drug Dangers
ISBN 0-7660-1157-7

Steroid Drug Dangers
ISBN 0-7660-1154-2

Tobacco and Nicotine Drug Dangers
ISBN 0-7660-1317-0

Tranquilizer, Barbiturate, and Downer
Drug Dangers
ISBN 0-7660-1320-0

one

Joe's Story

Joe was a typical teen. His dad described his oldest son as "a very sweet, very funny kid."[1] Joe played guitar. With his friends, he had formed a rock band. He also loved to write articles for his high school newspaper. He had won a statewide journalism award while a high school student in New Hampshire.

His parents said that Joe was not a reckless person. For example, Joe had said no to a family rafting trip through the Grand Canyon when he was seventeen years old. Instead, the whole family went sailing and played miniature golf.

Yet just a year later, Joe took LSD. Compared to rafting, "he figured that wasn't as dangerous," said his dad.[2]

At age eighteen, Joe started going to the University of Wisconsin in Madison. He lived on campus, in a seventh-floor dorm room. Just after classes began in September, Joe and a friend went to a rock concert near Milwaukee, Wisconsin. There, he got LSD and took his first trip, or had his first LSD experience.

In early October, Joe spent the weekend with his dad and stepmother. His dad remembered, "He was upbeat, funny, and full of his new activities, including fencing. He did a whole bunch of very impressive lunges and parries for us."

On October 15, Joe spent the evening with friends. After his friends left his dorm room, Joe again took LSD. This time, the drug made Joe think he could fly.[3] A little after one o'clock that Sunday morning, someone

LSD in a variety of forms is shown here. No matter how it is used, it can have deadly consequences.

studying across the dorm courtyard saw a curtain open. The student said a body fell out.

That body was Joe. As he fell, Joe did not cry out or make any noise, but he died immediately when he hit the ground seven stories below his dorm window. Joe's mother had warned him about LSD. Joe had told her about a friend who had taken it. "Obviously, he didn't listen to her advice," said his dad. "Kids think they're invulnerable [can live forever]. They're wrong."[4]

two

Society and Hallucinogens

People have used hallucinogens since ancient times. These drugs, or chemical substances, are also called psychoactive, mind-altering, and psychedelics. They have various names because of their powerful abilities. Hallucinogens alter perception of time and distance, thinking, mood, and behavior.

Cycles of Hallucinogen Use

During the 1960s, some Americans experimented with hallucinogens, but few became regular users. People used these drugs for their so-called mind-expanding potential. These drugs were believed to give the users special insights that they would not have otherwise. The most common of these drugs was lysergic acid diethylamide, or LSD. Mescaline and psilocybin were also used. These last two drugs have long been associated with religious ceremonies in various cultures.

LSD was used by millions of young adults in the 1960s. Many users were in their twenties. The abuse of hallucinogens became a major public health concern during this time. Why was there a concern?

Hallucinogens can produce unpredictable, erratic, and violent behavior in users. Sometimes the unruly behavior leads to injuries and death. Drowning, burns, falls, and traffic accidents can also result. The newspapers, radio, and television news ran story after story about LSD users who had injured or killed themselves. LSD use eventually dropped during the next decade.

According to federal drug officials, LSD use peaked in the 1970s. Then it went into decline. However, it never completely went away.[1] Hallucinogens, especially LSD, started to become popular again in the 1990s. Annual national surveys show that since 1991, LSD use has

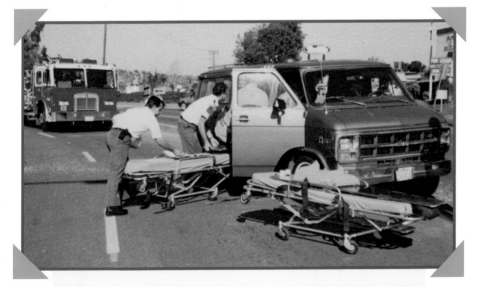

Hallucinogens such as LSD can cause the user to exhibit unpredictable behavior. At times such behavior can lead to traffic accidents or other unintended injuries.

increased. The number of hospital emergency room visits due to LSD has also steadily climbed.

Who Takes Hallucinogens and Why?

Today it is teens—in high school and junior high—who are using hallucinogens such as LSD. The Drug Enforcement Administration (DEA) reported that LSD is the fastest-growing drug of abuse among the under-twenty age group.[2]

According to the University of Michigan Monitoring the Future study, use of all hallucinogens leveled in 1997.[3] This news is good. The Monitoring the Future study surveys some fifty-one thousand students across the country. It has been carried out for twenty-three years. The results from the 1997 survey are below.

Former drug user Bob (not his real name) explained why he took LSD. "Most people couldn't tell when I was using. Kids would take LSD while in the classroom and the teacher never knew. You can easily get it and it's cheap. One hit costs from one to five dollars. Plus, there

Hallucinogen Use in the United States[4]

1997 students reporting any use of . . .	Percent	Grade
LSD in the 12 months prior to the survey.	3.2	8
	6.7	10
	8.4	12
Any other hallucinogens in the 12 months prior to the survey.	1.8	8
	3.3	10
	4.6	12

are no telltale signs. No smoke, no drug paraphernalia [equipment]."[5]

He continued, "I think another reason LSD has increased is that most drug testing does not test for LSD. Besides, you don't need to take much acid to get high. So, even if tested, most drug tests can't pick up such a tiny amount."[6]

Other teens say they take LSD because they are bored, they want to get high, they want to experiment, or because they are curious about its effects. Peer pressure plays a part in drug use, too. Young people can pressure their friends and classmates into trying drugs.

Experts point to even more reasons for the increase in the use of hallucinogens. One possible reason is society's renewed interest in the 1960s. Teens listen to 1960s music and read magazines and watch movies from that era. Even tie-dyed fashions from the 1960s are again popular.

The growth of rave clubs or parties is another factor in the resurgence of LSD use. Rave clubs are all-night dance and party clubs where drug taking, including hallucinogens, is common.

Other experts say that the low cost of LSD is upping its use. Low-dose LSD is readily available. Because LSD is so strong, only a tiny amount—30 to 50 micrograms, which is smaller than the amount that could fit on the head of a pin—can affect someone.

Another factor in LSD use is that today's preteens and teens seem to have little or no knowledge of the often devastating effects and aftereffects of hallucinogens.[7] They have forgotten or were never told about the accidents and deaths that result from the bizarre behavior associated with the use of hallucinogens.

Dr. Herbert D. Kleber, a former White House

The growth of rave clubs, or places where teens can go to all-night dance parties, appears to be a factor in the recent increase in the popularity of LSD use.

specialist on drug treatment and education, said that hallucinogen use seems to run in cycles. At first, "people say, 'Hey, this must be a safe drug.' More people start using it and the casualties [accidents and deaths] start increasing. Sooner or later people say, 'Hey, this is a really dangerous drug.' The numbers drop and in a few years no one in their high school has gotten into trouble. It's like each new generation has to learn that, indeed, this [hallucinogens] can be a dangerous drug."[8]

Booming Black Market

Users get hallucinogens in illegal ways. The heavy demand for these drugs has created a black, or illegal, market. According to the Drug Enforcement

Administration (DEA), most of the illegal American LSD is made in San Francisco.[9]

Teens can easily get hallucinogens. Because these drugs are not controlled by the federal government, however, they may be fake. They may also be cut, or laced, with other harmful drugs or substances. There is no way for most people to know the purity or strength of what they are getting when they buy hallucinogens. This makes taking hallucinogens quite risky.

The Law

During the late 1960s, several laws were passed that made the sale of LSD illegal. In 1970, Congress passed a law popularly called the Controlled Substances Act (CSA). All hallucinogens were placed under this law.

This law makes it illegal to manufacture (make), possess, or sell hallucinogens. If caught, the person can receive stiff sentences: spend five or more years in prison, and pay heavy fines. These penalties hold true in all states and the District of Columbia. Hallucinogens are CSA Schedule I drugs, meaning that hallucinogens are at the top of the controlled substances list. Hallucinogen users or dealers will get the most severe penalties under the law.

Schedule I drugs such as hallucinogens

- ◆ have a high potential for abuse;
- ◆ present an unacceptable safety risk; and
- ◆ have no acceptable medical use.

LSD is the most commonly used hallucinogen. The actual prison terms and fines for use depend on whether

It is illegal to manufacture, possess, or sell hallucinogens. If caught, prison terms and heavy fines can be expected. This person is being finger printed before going to jail.

or not the user has been caught before with LSD and the amount of LSD involved.

Look for Signs

Unless you know what to look for, hallucinogen use is sometimes hard to spot. Here are some warnings signs.

Warning Signs

- ◆ anxiety, panic, confusion
- ◆ dilated or enlarged pupils
- ◆ distorted sense of time, space, and reality
- ◆ dry mouth
- ◆ hallucinations

- increased body temperature, heart rate, blood pressure
- loss of appetite
- sleeping problems
- sudden mood swings
- sweating
- tremors or body shaking
- violent behavior

Unpredictable Actions

Taking hallucinogens can indirectly lead to injury or death. Injury or death can happen because of the drug's powerful mind-altering effects, including loss of control and distorted perception. An LSD trip can lead users to misjudge distances or danger. Someone, like Joe (from the first chapter), may attempt to "fly" out of a window while on LSD, for example.

People under the influence of hallucinogens can cause themselves or others physical harm. These drugs

Penalties for LSD Use

Illegal Act	Federal Penalty
First time someone is caught making or distributing LSD.	Five to forty years in prison and up to $2 million fine.
Second time someone is caught making or distributing LSD.	Ten years to life in prison and from $2 million to $8 million fine.
If caught using LSD.	One to two years in prison.

can produce unpredictable or even violent behavior. In turn, this can lead to serious injuries and even death.

One former LSD user remembered, "I stuck my hand in this flame and then I went 'Uh-oh, my hand is in the flame,' and I pulled it out and I thought it didn't burn, but later that night, my hand started blistering."[10]

The use of hallucinogens, and the resulting unpredictable behavior, has caused drowning, burns, falls, and traffic accidents. Here are some statistics about the consequences of using hallucinogens:

- ◆ Every year, over ten thousand people end up in the hospital emergency room with LSD-related problems.[11]

- ◆ Hospital emergency rooms report a 100 percent increase in LSD-related admissions since 1985.[12]

The use of hallucinogens, and the unpredictable behavior that follows, can lead to serious injuries. Users have been known to burn themselves because they were unable to recognize the potential danger of a fire.

◆ Every year, several hundred people die as a result of LSD use.[13]

Panic attacks are common with hallucinogens, as are flashbacks. Flashbacks are effects that continue to occur long after drug use is discontinued. Days or even weeks after taking LSD, a user can still have a flashback, and jump from a window or turn against a friend. Hallucinations (seeing and hearing things that are not really there) are also common. Hallucinogens can cause users to go into convulsions (have fits or seizures) or become violent. In 1991, for example, a college student in Texas shot three friends after using LSD, and a Virginia teen shot a county police officer.[14]

Taking hallucinogens is risky. Everyone reacts differently to them. No one can predict if a user will have a good trip or a bad trip.

Hallucinogens Can Cause These Changes in a User:

◆ a sense of distance or not being involved or belonging with friends, family, and others;

◆ depression, anxiety, and paranoia;

◆ violent behavior;

◆ confusion, suspicion, and loss of control;

◆ flashbacks; and

◆ a catatonic state. Users cannot talk or connect with the real world. They become very tired and disoriented and constantly repeat motions that have no meaning.

three

Real-Life Stories

Here are some stories about real people who used hallucinogens.

Bob and Sam

Bob (not his real name) is a former drug user. He and his younger brother, Sam (not his real name), took LSD a number of times while they were in high school. Sometimes their LSD trips or experiences were frightening. According to Bob,

> We would take LSD on a Friday or Saturday night up in our bedroom. We shared a bedroom. The LSD would keep us up all night long. We couldn't sleep. We'd still be up at 10 o'clock the next morning.
>
> We'd take a tiny little pill or lick a small piece of paper with acid [another name for LSD]. First I'd feel like I had a bunch of electricity coursing through my body. But, as my acid trip

[LSD experience] went on, late at night, the good feelings started to shift to negative feelings. LSD intensified any negative feelings I had. For instance, if something was irritating me, the acid made it much worse. I remember punching my brother because he wouldn't change the radio station we were listening to. I didn't like the song that was on. He did. I punched him so hard that he had a big bruise on his arm the next day.

Bob continued,

LSD's effects are very dependent on your mood and setting. My brother and I usually took it at the same time. We'd stay in our bedroom or in the immediate area. I couldn't make many decisions while on acid, or I'd feel overwhelmed. Taking acid made it seem that going through the motions of daily life was a huge labor. Just getting dressed felt like it was really hard to to. It seemed to take forever. Going through simple actions was so complicated. I would wonder if it was worth the effort putting on my socks and shoes, for example.

Sam and I knew LSD was a powerful drug. We always took small doses of it. Even so, the effects would last twelve to fourteen hours, which is typical. But it wasn't worth it. We were tired and angry the next day. Just getting up and getting dressed was exhausting. So, I'd stay home from school and miss out on tests and playing basketball after school.[1]

Hallucinogen in Toads' Poison

Bob Shepard was a teacher at a nature center. He dried and smoked bufotenine. This illegal hallucinogen is found in the venom (poison) of Colorado River toads. When arrested for the possession of bufotenine, Shepard told police that he used the venom. When asked why, he said he wanted to help others understand the powers of this drug.[2]

Blotter paper, a form of LSD shown here, can be licked and comes with a variety of patterns on it.

LSD and School Do Not Mix

One teen found out that LSD and school do not mix. The drug disabled the control needed to function at school. He said:

> I was tripping [on LSD] in school and you can't work in school, 'cause you look at the letters and they fall off the pages. And you try to pick them back up, but it doesn't work. I remember being in geometry class once, taking a test, and I couldn't remember any of it. And like the words and like images on the paper were like scrambling and stuff, and like, there was stuff coming out of the paper. . . . My friend said I was like writing in the air and stuff, and it was just really crazy.[3]

Another teen explained why he could not do schoolwork while high on LSD. "You see the same words over and over and the words fall off the page. You can't trip and go to school."[4]

Arrested for Crazy Behavior While on LSD

Three friends had taken LSD. They were outside, in a field. One of the friends had taken his clothes off. Here is what happened next:

> Somebody saw him running around naked and called the cops. And the cops came. I remember sitting in the middle of the field. There was a cop walking out toward me; I was just sitting there. He had his gun drawn, and he was moving back and forth like this, so there was a whole row of him in three different colors. . . . It didn't occur to me when I saw the pretty blue and red lights that something was happening. I remember seeing them beat my best friend. It scared me a lot. Then when we got arrested—I just, I didn't know what was happening to me at all.[5]

Timothy Leary, LSD Guru

Timothy Leary, self-professed guru of drug use, promoted the use of hallucinogens from 1960 until his death on May 31, 1996, at seventy-five years old. Leary got a Ph.D. in psychology from West Point. He was then hired as a psychology professor at Harvard University in Cambridge, Massachusetts. During a visit to Mexico in 1960, he tried his first hallucinogen: psilocybin mushrooms. Next he tried mescaline. The drug, according to Leary, "was freely available by mail order from several New York pharmaceutical houses."[6] Today we know the dangers associated with the use of this illegal hallucinogen.

In the spring of 1962, Leary took LSD for the first time. He described it as "the most shattering experience of my life."[7] Leary believed that hallucinogens were "the key to increased intelligence."[8] He began testing LSD and other hallucinogens on his students but was soon fired from Harvard.

Leary was then supposed to conduct research on hallucinogens. But he never ran any scientific experiments. Instead, he encouraged friends and others to take hallucinogens. In 1966 he was arrested on drug charges. After three years in prison, however, he continued to use hallucinogens.

Some people were not sad when Leary died in 1996. Said Daniel Addario, who helped bring drug charges against Leary, "He was evil. I've seen what LSD can do to people."[9]

When he heard of Leary's death, comedian and television star Art Linkletter said, "You could only call it 'what goes around comes around.'" Linkletter's daughter, age twenty, had jumped to her death during a 1969 acid (LSD) trip.[10]

Scary Experience While on PCP

Some teens and young adults go to dance clubs where they take drugs. The drugs get the dancers high and supposedly increase their energy. One teen went with his friends to a dance club in New York City. He took some candy that contained PCP. PCP is a powerful hallucinogen that can cause strange and bizarre thoughts and behavior.

The teen soon realized that his "high was a little

different this time." Then, while standing in the lounge eating a peach, he seemed to have lost his right arm.[11]

> It freaked me out, because my arm just wasn't there. This strange arm with the peach kept coming up to my mouth and I'd take a bite, and then it would go down again. I turned to my girlfriend and told her, "please don't laugh at me too much, but I can't find my right arm." She started laughing when I said that, but I was getting really scared, because here was this strange arm coming up to my mouth all the time, and I couldn't find my arm anywhere. . . ."[12]

World's First LSD Experience

The first recorded LSD experience, which took place in 1943, was an accident. Swiss chemist Albert Hoffman was working with LSD in his laboratory. Somehow, he absorbed a bit of it. Suddenly, he felt dizzy and could not concentrate. He had hallucinations, or imaginary sights, sounds, smells, and other sensations. He went home to rest. Then he remembered that he went into "a peculiar state similar to drunkenness, characterized by an exaggerated imagination."[13]

Hoffman decided to take more of the drug to see what would happen. He took 250 micrograms (which is smaller than the amount that could fit on the head of a pin, but about five to ten times the amount needed for an LSD reaction). At first, he started to carefully write down his reactions in his laboratory book. But after forty minutes, he stopped writing. His last words were barely legible. Hoffman then asked his lab technician to take him home.[14] Hoffman thought he was losing his mind.

four

Dangers of Hallucinogens

Hallucinogens are powerful, psychoactive drugs. Psychoactive drugs affect the central nervous system and interfere with normal brain function. They represent a diverse group of substances, including both factory-made drugs and naturally occurring plants. People take these illegal drugs to alter their perceptions and thinking patterns.

After decades of research, scientists have uncovered no accepted medical use for hallucinogens. They are not used medically in the United States. The problems associated with hallucinogens far outweigh any possible benefits.

History

Going back to ancient history, hallucinogenic mushrooms were eaten in India in 1500 B.C. and pre-Columbian Mexico in A.D. 100. Poisonous ergot was accidentally eaten in Renaissance Europe. Ergot is found in rye mold, a natural form of LSD. In the past, hundreds of primitive tribes in the Americas, such as the Aztecs and Toltecs, used dozens of hallucinogenic plants, including peyote, psilocybin, and morning glory seeds. They took these hallucinogenic plants for social, ceremonial, and medical reasons.

Today, some tribes still use hallucinogenic plants for the same reasons. Hallucinogens use can still be found throughout the world. Currently, most of these drugs are grown, made, or used in the Americas and Africa. The first major wave of hallucinogen use hit America during the 1960s and into the 1970s. The second wave occurred during the 1990s.

In the past, the Aztecs and Toltecs used dozens of hallucinogenic plants for a variety of social, ceremonial, and medical reasons. The ceremonial drug use was often reflected in their art.

Hallucinogens Defined

Hallucinogens change the user's mood, behavior, mental functioning, and perception. Perception occurs when someone becomes aware of one's surroundings, using the senses—especially sight and hearing. Hallucinogens distort moods, thoughts, and the senses, including sight, touch, smell, and hearing. They do this by overloading the brain stem. The brain stem is the sensory switchboard for the mind. When the brain stem is overloaded, it causes the brain to mix up and intensify sensations. That is why users sometimes have hallucinations, or imaginary sights, sounds, and smells. Hallucinations are not always good experiences and can be very frightening. These drugs also increase heart and breathing rates. They can harm judgment and reasoning, causing users to make unwise, sometimes dangerous, decisions.

The distorted mental states caused by hallucinogens can last for many hours or several days. The effects are very unpredictable. Users sometimes have harmed themselves physically. Or they have behaved violently toward others. If users mix hallucinogens with other drugs, serious mental or emotional problems can result. Every year thousands of people end up in the hospital emergency room because hallucinogen use has

   ◆ triggered serious mental problems in users;

   ◆ caused users to hurt themselves; and

   ◆ caused users to hurt other people.

Types of Hallucinogens

There are two types of hallucinogens: those that are artificially made and those that come from plants. Here is a summary of the two types:

Artificially-Made Hallucinogens

Lysergic acid diethylamide (LSD)
A very powerful hallucinogen. It stimulates the body by increasing the action of the central nervous system, the heart, and other organs.

Phencyclidine (PCP)
Also called angel dust. It deadens sensations and causes users to close themselves off from their surroundings and senses.

Hallucinogenic Plants

Peyote and Mescaline
Mescaline, a naturally occurring chemical found in the peyote cactus, causes vivid hallucinations and nausea. It stimulates the body by increasing the action of the central nervous system, the heart, and other organs.

Psilocybin and Psilocin
Poisonous mushrooms contain psilocybin. This substance causes hallucinations, nausea, and sometimes vomiting.

The History of LSD

LSD was created in a lab in Switzerland in 1938. It originally was found in ergot, a fungus that grows on rye and other grains. At that time, chemists were trying to develop new drugs to cure headaches. It was not until 1943, though, that a Swiss chemist named Albert Hoffmann accidentally discovered LSD's mind-altering properties.

After the discovery of LSD, researchers tested the drug to see if it could help people with headaches and

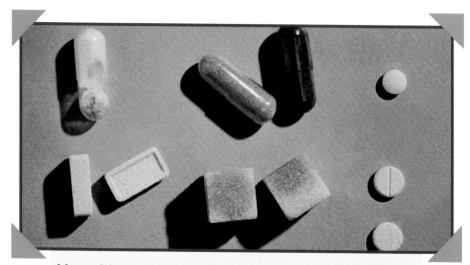

Many of the street names for LSD come from the different forms that the drug comes in. Some of those forms are shown here.

other health problems. But after a couple of decades, researchers found LSD medically useless, and they stopped all LSD studies.

By 1960 the use of LSD for its mind-altering properties had moved from researchers in their labs to young people in their twenties. Many of these young adults called themselves flower children or hippies. They wanted a different world of peace and love. Many thought LSD would give them special insights into finding and creating this world, which they thought they could enjoy without ever being part of mainstream society.

LSD soon developed a bad reputation. Thousands of young people were hurt or killed while on a bad LSD trip, or experience. As a result, the federal government declared LSD an illegal drug in 1966. Since then, the only source of LSD has been illegal, on the streets. LSD use plunged then resurfaced during the 1990s.

LSD is a synthetic, an artificially made form of a

poison that infects rye. A toxin is a poison. Pure LSD is odorless and colorless. It tastes slightly bitter. This drug has many street names. Here are some of them.

Effects

LSD produces detachment (a feeling of separation and disconnection) and euphoria, an exaggerated feeling of happiness and well-being. It also heightens feelings, from joy to sadness. LSD intensifies vision. It often leads to a crossing of senses in which colors appear to be heard and sounds appear to be seen. Users have reported that the drug seems to slow the passage of time and produce a dreamlike feeling.

The drug may produce feelings of anxiety and panic. LSD can also create a feeling of lack of self-control and extreme terror.

Physical Effects from Taking LSD

- ◆ dilated pupils
- ◆ dizziness
- ◆ drowsiness

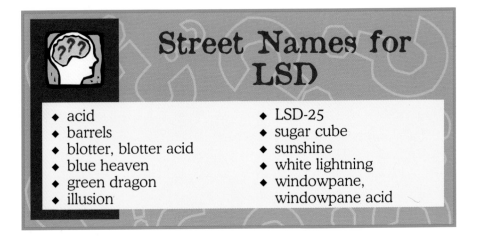

Street Names for LSD

- ◆ acid
- ◆ barrels
- ◆ blotter, blotter acid
- ◆ blue heaven
- ◆ green dragon
- ◆ illusion

- ◆ LSD-25
- ◆ sugar cube
- ◆ sunshine
- ◆ white lightning
- ◆ windowpane, windowpane acid

- flushed or red face
- goose bumps
- nausea
- numbness and tingling
- rise in body temperature
- sweating
- tremors
- weakness

Bad LSD experiences, or bad trips, are unpredictable. A bad trip can occur even among those who had a so-called good trip in the past. Bad trips generally are not related to the amount of LSD taken. Rather, the user's personality, the setting in which use occurs, and the quality and origin of the drug play more important roles in shaping the drug trip. One former user said his final trip "oozed with evil and horrifying visions worse than any nightmare that could be imagined."[1]

The day after LSD use, a long and uncomfortable period of depression, much like an alcoholic hangover, follows.

How LSD Is Used

According to the American Council for Drug Education, LSD is used mostly by white, middle-class teens who live in cities and suburbs.[3] Some of these teens take other drugs such as marijuana, alcohol, or tobacco. Others only use LSD.

Teens can also take LSD by accident. At some parties, the punch may be spiked with LSD. These jokes may result in a trip to the emergency room. For many teens, raves are the first time they run across LSD. Dealers at raves claim that the drug expands the mind and enhances the effect of the dance lights and lasers.

How LSD Is Sold

Because LSD is so potent, only small amounts are needed. It is usually sold in tablets or in liquid form. Sometimes it is absorbed into a sugar cube or other substance.

Blotter Acid

Users chew, lick, or swallow small sheets of blotter paper that have liquid LSD on them. Blotter paper contains a series of small, colorful, stamped drawings. The drawings vary, and each one is suppose to contain one dose of LSD.

Microdots

LSD comes in tiny tablets or capsules.

Windowpanes

LSD comes in thin, gelatin squares.

Other

LSD can also be found on candy, sugar cubes, aspirin, jewelry, liquor, cloth, and on the back of postage stamps. It can also be injected, but this is less common than taking it by mouth.

PCP

Phencyclidine (PCP) is a powerful hallucinogen. It is a public health concern because it can be cheaply and easily made in home laboratories. Like LSD, it is illegal and has many names. Note that two names for PCP, ice and krystal, are also street names for methamphetamine, also called meth. Some users may end up with PCP

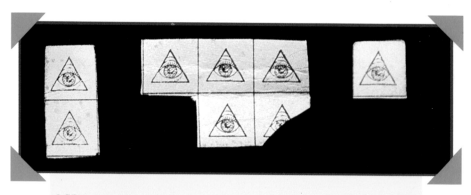

LSD users may chew, lick, or swallow small sheets of blotter paper such as the ones shown here. Blotter paper is generally covered with liquid LSD.

instead of meth. The unexpected results can be dangerous for the users.

PCP comes in liquid, crystal, or powder form. It is often smoked or sprinkled on a marijuana joint or cigarette. It can also be snorted through the nose, swallowed, or injected. One former PCP user said, "If you smoke it, depending on how strong the joint is, you just kind of get a floating sensation about one minute after you take your first few tokes [puffs]. And you just get a really numbed sensation."[4]

History

PCP was introduced in the 1950s as an animal tranquilizer. (Tranquilizers relax the user by reducing muscle activity, coordination, and attention span.) Because of its serious side effects, PCP could not be used as an anesthetic for people. After a few years, however, dealers began to sell illegal PCP. They billed it as a substitute for hallucinogens such as LSD and mescaline. In the late 1970s, PCP became a common drug of abuse.

Then its use declined. PCP resurfaced in the 1990s as a popular hallucinogen.

Effects

PCP affects the central nervous system. Its effects are quite different from those of other hallucinogens. PCP produces a sense of detachment and reduces sensitivity to pain. This combination sometimes results in weird thinking. Some users also become violent and destructive.

Said one former PCP user,

> I've had seizures before on it and banged my head really hard—continually, on hard objects—and got lots of bumps and everything and felt them the next few days but never realized I was doing it and never felt hurt from it.[5]

PCP disturbs the normal identification that a person has with his or her body parts. When a normal person looks at his hand, he knows that the hand is part of his body. Most people take this sense of self-identity for

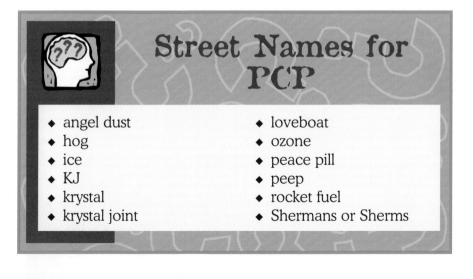

Street Names for PCP

- angel dust
- hog
- ice
- KJ
- krystal
- krystal joint
- loveboat
- ozone
- peace pill
- peep
- rocket fuel
- Shermans or Sherms

granted. But someone on PCP may look at his or her own hand and not realize it belongs to the body.

Because PCP causes long-lasting numbness throughout the body, the person could do harmful things and not feel them. Examples of bizarre behavior while on PCP include, "pulling out one's teeth with pliers, setting fire to oneself, stabbings, or assaults."[6] Another bizarre behavior occurred when the user bit his own forearms "almost to the bone."[7]

Using PCP can result in another big problem. The drug can either trigger or produce symptoms that are so similar to those of schizophrenia that even experts confuse the two states. Schizophrenia is a mental disorder in which a person loses awareness of reality and the ability to relate closely with others. Someone with schizophrenia often has disturbed behavior and cannot reason well.

There is no way to predict when a bad PCP trip, or experience, will happen. Bizarre and violent behavior can occur with small or large doses.[8] The effects of a small dose of PCP can last one to two hours. The effects of a large dose can last much longer, up to forty-eight hours.

Compared with other hallucinogens, users of PCP have more sharply contrasting responses to the drug. Its effects vary greatly from user to user. The drug can either stimulate or depress the central nervous system. Such unpredictability makes PCP a dangerous psychoactive drug. PCP greatly effects thinking, time perception, sense of reality, and mood.

The drug produces dreamlike states, euphoria (exaggerated feeling of happiness) or depression, and bizarre perceptions. Users also can develop severe loss of

Using PCP

Taking PCP Just Once Can Cause

- anxiety;
- confusion;
- disorientation;
- hostility and anger;
- irritability;
- paranoia;
- violent behavior; and

- death due to convulsions, heart or lung failure, exploded blood vessels in the brain, or the destructive behavior that this drug produces.

Using PCP Repeatedly

- decreases the ability to remember specific facts;
- impairs speech;
- impairs judgment and concentration long after users stop taking the drug;
- produces anxiety,

depression, violent behavior; and
- can result in mental problems such as depression. Users sometimes need professional or institutional care.

orientation with their surroundings, distorted time and space, and inability to feel pain. Their emotions become altered.

Taking PCP can cause users to become extremely hostile and violent. This behavior can lead to death resulting from drowning, burns, falls, and traffic accidents. In fact, more people die from the results of bizarre behavior produced by PCP than by the drug's direct effects of on the body.[9]

One Los Angeles police officer called PCP "stronger and more dangerous than LSD." He rated PCP as the worst of the commonly abused hallucinogens.[10]

PCP remains in the body for a long time, even days. Flashbacks can occur at any time. They can cause panic, confusion, suspicion, and lack of control. Flashbacks can also repeat unpleasant physical and visual feelings.

Ketamine

Ketamine is a drug that is closely related to PCP. Ketamine was originally used as an anesthetic for people, to numb the body. But its effects were very unpredictable, and it is no longer used to treat people. Like PCP, ketamine is a legal drug. It is available by prescription for use by veterinarians. According to the Drug Enforcement Administration (DEA), ketamine is being abused by an increasing number of teens and young adults as a club drug.[11] It is often distributed at raves and other parties.

When people use ketamine, they go into a dreamlike state, often filled with hallucinations. They feel no physical pain. This state can last up to six hours. Like PCP, ketamine use can result in coma, convulsions, and violent behavior.

Ketamine Can Cause

- ◆ confusion;
- ◆ detachment from environment;
- ◆ dizziness;
- ◆ hallucinations;
- ◆ muscle rigidity;
- ◆ poor coordination;
- ◆ slurred speech;

- ◆ violent behavior; and
- ◆ death due to choking, breathing failure, convulsions, or coma.

One user of ketamine was Dr. John Lilly. A neuroscientist, Lilly pioneered communication with dolphins. He said that a medical doctor gave him ketamine in the 1970s for severe migraine headaches. Lilly started to take the drug, by injection, on his own. While on ketamine, he became convinced "that he was a visitor from the year 3001" and that he was talking to aliens.[12]

Like Lilly, ketamine users often inject the drug. But others swallow, smoke, or snort it.

Peyote and Mescaline

Peyote is the name for a small, spineless, turnip-shaped cactus. This cactus is native to Mexico and the

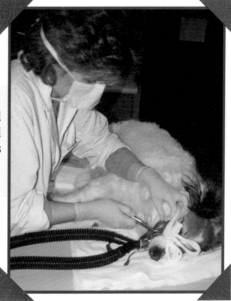

Ketamine is a drug intended for use as an animal anesthesia. Its formula is closely related to that of PCP

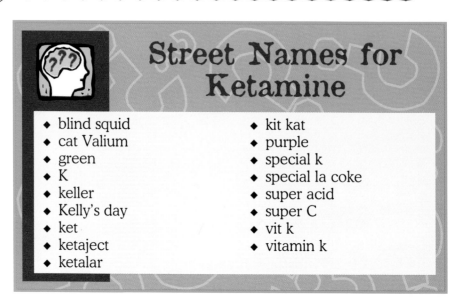

Street Names for Ketamine

- blind squid
- cat Valium
- green
- K
- keller
- Kelly's day
- ket
- ketaject
- ketalar
- kit kat
- purple
- special k
- special la coke
- super acid
- super C
- vit k
- vitamin k

southwestern United States. The tops of the peyote cactus yield mescaline, a hallucinogen.

The mushroom-shaped tops called peyote, or mescal buttons, are grayish. The fresh or dried buttons are eaten, brewed into a tea, powdered, or packaged into capsules. Synthetic or artificially made mescaline is a thin, needlelike crystal. Pure mescaline has no color and tastes bitter. It is usually sold in capsules or tablets.

When sold on the street, mescaline is often impure. The capsules or tablets may not contain any mescaline or only small amounts. Other drugs such as PCP or LSD are sometimes passed off as mescaline. Unexpected results from these other drugs can be dangerous for users.

History

Since pre-Columbian times, American Indians have used peyote in their religious ceremonies. Its use is recorded in ancient writings of the Aztecs. When the Spaniards invaded the New World, they thought the use of peyote was evil.[13] They believed that the hallucinations from taking peyote came from the devil.[14] The Spaniards tried to ban the use of peyote, but never succeeded.

Instead, the use of peyote spread. By the early 1900s, about fifty North American tribes were using it. Today peyote cacti are still eaten by some northern Mexican tribes and by the Southwest Plains American Indian tribes. Also, the Native American Church of North America uses peyote for religious purposes.

It is legal for American Indians to use peyote in religious ceremonies. This use is protected under the American Indian Religious Freedom Act Amendments of 1994. All other use, sales, possession, or manufacture of peyote or mescaline is illegal.

Peyote cactus, native to Mexico and the southwestern United States, is known for its hallucinogenic properties.

Effects

Compared with synthetic hallucinogens, pure plant peyote has a slow onset. It can take forty minutes to two hours before the effects begin. The effects last a long time, from ten to twelve hours.

The drug's effects are similar to LSD. Mescaline, though, produces more vivid and colorful hallucinations compared to LSD. When people take peyote, they often become extremely nauseated and vomit. As with most hallucinogens, tolerance to the mental effects of mescaline can develop quickly.

Effects of Peyote and Mescaline

- altered perception and sense of time
- colorful hallucinations
- confusion
- dizziness
- feelings of anxiety, disorientation
- feelings of elation or depression
- headaches
- increase in heart rate and blood pressure, rise in body temperature
- nausea
- sweating
- vomiting

Psilocybin and Psilocin

Hallucinogenic mushrooms grow naturally in many parts of the world. The active ingredients in most of these mushrooms are psilocybin or psilocin. Hallucinogenic mushrooms go by a variety of names: magic mushrooms, shrooms, and sacred mushrooms.

When sold on the street, many users do not get hallucinogenic mushrooms. Instead, the mushrooms may come from the grocery store. Dealers then freeze them, and spike them with LSD or PCP. Unexpected results from these other drugs can be dangerous for users. Because many mushrooms that grow in the wild are poisonous, picking hallucinogenic mushrooms is dangerous.

History

Hallucinogenic mushrooms were important to Indian cultures in parts of Mexico and Central America. Their use among cultures in these areas has been traced to 1,500 B.C. Scientists believe that mushroom use was widespread.[15] They have found stone images of mushrooms carved into the shape of a god from 1,000 B.C. in Guatemala. The first recorded use occurred during the crowning of Montezuma in 1502. These mushrooms are still used today by some descendants of those people.

In the 1950s, Albert Hoffmann (the discoverer of LSD) researched hallucinogenic mushrooms. Hoffman discovered how to make psilocybin and psilocin synthetically. Psilocybin and psilocin were then used by writers, painters, and entertainers during the 1950s and 1960s. Today, the use, sale, possession, or manufacture of psilocybin, psilocyn, or hallucinogenic mushrooms is illegal.

Effects

Hallucinogenic mushrooms can be eaten raw. They can also be dried, stewed, or put into soup or drinks. Both

Hallucinogenic mushrooms grow naturally in many parts of the world. Users who buy them on the street, however, may get only store-bought mushrooms that have been laced with PCP or LSD.

wild and home-grown mushrooms vary greatly in strength.

When users take these mushrooms, they often feel queasy and may vomit. Then the mental effects, which are somewhat like those of LSD, take over. They can last four to six hours. Similar to LSD, the effects of hallucinogenic mushrooms are unpredictable and depend a lot on the setting. The setting includes the surroundings, other people, and mood of the user.

Effects of Psilocybin and Psilocin

- ◆ altered perception and sense of time and space
- ◆ depression
- ◆ dizziness
- ◆ hallucinations
- ◆ impaired judgment
- ◆ inappropriate laughter

- increase in heart rate, blood pressure, and body temperature

- nausea

- poisoning

- tiredness

- tolerance

- vomiting

Bob took magic mushrooms once.

It was early June in California. I was with some friends on a beach. The shrooms tasted terrible. Then we went swimming in the Pacific Ocean. Three- and four-foot waves were coming in. Because of the drug's effects, the waves looked like gigantic tidal waves. I was scared, so I got out [of the water] and tried to play a game of Frisbee™ with one of my friends. We couldn't throw that Frisbee straight, no matter how hard we tried. We gave up after I hit a woman in the head. It must have hurt, as I threw that Frisbee hard.[16]

Some mushroom users have had flashbacks that cause panic, confusion, suspicion, and lack of control. Flashbacks can also repeat unpleasant physical and visual feelings.

five

Fighting

Drug Abuse

Two keys in combating the use of hallucinogens are awareness and education. Federal drug programs, national organizations, schools, communities, and individuals provide information, education, and help in dealing with these drugs.

Federal Government

The Department of Health and Human Services launched a national public education campaign in the late 1990s. Called Girl Power!, the program helps preteen and young teen girls make the most of their lives. The program maintains a Web site on the National Clearinghouse for Alcohol and Drug Information (NCADI) at <http://www.health .org>. Girls can help build the Web site. All they need to do is join the Girl Power! construction team. They can put their ideas on the forms posted on the Web site, then click the "SEND IT NOW!" button. Or they can send their ideas by mail to Girl Power!

At this Web site teens can

- find links to other Internet sites for girls;
- find out which cheers won the Girl Power! cheer contest;
- get a message from Girl Power! spokesperson and gymnast Dominique Dawes;
- get tips on how to get Girl Power! materials; and
- learn the facts about drugs.

Schools

Schools provide a great way to teach kids about the dangers of hallucinogens and other drugs. Here are programs in two schools:

All Stars

One example of working through the schools is the All Stars program. The program was first tested in seventh-grade classes in Lexington, North Carolina. This program helps teens learn how to enhance positive traits or characteristics, and prevent drug abuse.

All Stars uses fourteen classroom sessions to teach students that high-risk behavior, such as taking drugs, is actually rare. Such behavior will interfere with their desired lifestyles, too. There is an "at home" portion. All Stars asks parents to get involved with the program. It provides homework for the parents and gives them a chance to talk about drug issues with their teens.

To help teens make personal commitments and avoid high-risk behavior, the program asks them to fill out personal commitment forms. The forms must be signed by a parent or another adult. Teens write down their ideals and explain what they will do about drinking alcohol, smoking, using drugs, and having sex. The program includes exercises that let teens play in skits about drug abuse. The students then decide what behavior is best. At the end of the program, teens are awarded certificates. They also get silver rings.

LA's Best

This after-school enrichment program offers varied programs to five thousand students in twenty-four elementary schools in Los Angeles, California. Fifty schools will eventually be part of this program.

Activities include tutoring, sports, arts, crafts, theater, field trips, and computer training. The Los Angeles Unified School District runs the program every day from the end of school until 6:00 P.M. Studies show that kids who are part of LA's Best like school more, show positive behavior changes, feel safer, improve their grades, and are less likely to take drugs or be involved in school-based crime.

Many states are also battling drug abuse in various ways. California and New Jersey are examples of what states are doing.

California's Mentoring Initiative

In 1995, Governor Pete Wilson believed so strongly in the power of mentoring that he created the California Mentoring Initiative.[1] This program was set up to provide role models to the thousands of kids who need them the most. This public/private partnership—the largest in the United States—uses resources of the state government, local community groups, and existing mentoring programs. The program links supportive caring role models with teens. A mentor, then, is a caring person

In an effort to provide positive role models for young people, the state of California started a mentoring program in 1995. Mentors provide one-on-one attention and support for teens.

who provides one-on-one support and attention to a teen. The mentor is a friend and role model. Such supportive role models can help teens see themselves in positive ways. All mentors are trained. They received training during the time they mentor.

Mentoring works. In 1995, Public/Private Ventures, a nonprofit organization, studied Big Brother/Big Sister (BB/BS) programs. BB/BS mentor teens. Researchers found that BB/BS programs have many positive effects on the lives of teens. Teens who had mentors were much less likely to start using alcohol and other drugs, were not absent from school as often, and got better grades.

The New Jersey Governor's Council on Alcohol and Drug Abuse

This program has taken the issues of drug abuse awareness and prevention statewide. Each year, twenty-one counties participate in National Drug Prevention and Awareness Week. John Kriger, chief of training, offers workshops to educate PTAs, police officers, and other groups about drug abuse. Kriger's program shows adults what to look for and how to handle drug abuse.

Communities

Various communities, local and national, are working to combat drug abuse. Here are some examples.

Parent Teacher Association (PTA)

For many years, this group has worked to increase public awareness about drug abuse. This education and parent organization has millions of members worldwide. The PTA encourages its members to hold drug abuse awareness workshops or meetings. Parents are welcome to attend. Nursing students from the local university and police officers have presented information and passed out information at these workshops and meetings.

Partnership for a Drug-Free America

This group has run many campaigns to tell the public about the dangers of drug abuse, including hallucinogens. Their campaigns distribute print and television warning ads to America's largest media markets. Partnership for a Drug-Free America is a volunteer organization of communications companies.

Poison Control Centers

Across the United States, these centers provide information on the problem of hallucinogen abuse. They can help evaluate various drugs and recommend the best treatment if used. Poison Control Centers are involved in informational and awareness prevention campaigns and programs that teach kids about drug safety.

The Elks

This society is located in nearly twenty-three hundred communities nationwide and counts more than one million members. The Elks National Drug Awareness Program "honors and educates young people who are willing to be part of the solution rather than part of the problem," said Andy Milwid, executive director.[2] The Elks drug prevention program provides material for fourth through seventh-grade students on various drugs, including hallucinogens. Students receive drug prevention brochures and coloring materials, and participate in poster contests aimed at prevention. Over 3 million kids in the United States have been part of the Elks "Hoop Shoot" Free Throw Contest. This contest is held each year.

Your Parents

You may have seen television ads that tell you to talk to your parents about drugs. It is a good idea. Some of today's parents may have used hallucinogens in their young adult years. No one is sure of the exact numbers of people who used hallucinogens in the 1960s and 1970s. But if parents did take these drugs, they may be embarrassed to tell their kids about it.

But this is exactly why teens today know so little about the problems associated with hallucinogens. Both parents and kids need to be honest and open. They need to talk about the dangers of drugs, including hallucinogens.

six

What You Can Do

Deciding what to put into the body is a very personal decision. But staying away from hallucinogens and other illegal drugs (and encouraging others to do the same) is always a safe, wise choice.

Saying No to Hallucinogens

It is not always easy to say no. Saying no to hallucinogens and other drugs sometimes takes courage. However, by refusing to use drugs, you show that you value yourself. You are also saying that you are responsible for what you do, and decide not to do.

Three Steps to Saying No to Drugs

When a friend wants to do something that might not be the right thing, follow these three steps in deciding what to do:

1. Figure out whether what that friend wants to do is acceptable. "Is this safe?" or "Will it cause trouble?" or "Would parents approve?" or "Would it feel right doing this?"

2. If the answer to any of those questions is no, say no or no thanks to the friend. When saying no, sound firm and confident. Shaking the head, folding arms across the chest, or putting hands in pockets are good, firm actions. These actions and the refusal tell the other person that the answer is definitely no.

3. Suggest other things to do that are fun and safe. Be upbeat and positive about your ideas.

If the friend persists, walk away.

Quitting

If someone wants to quit using hallucinogens or other drugs, he or she can talk to

- ◆ Alateen, a group with branches throughout the United States for teen friends and family members of drug abusers;
- ◆ a drug treatment program or a chemical dependency program;
- ◆ family or friends;
- ◆ hot lines and referral services;
- ◆ mental health agencies;
- ◆ drug abuse organizations in the area;
- ◆ teachers, school counselors, drug abuse counselors, physician, or other health professionals.

Tell Others About Hallucinogen Abuse

To help others get information about the dangers of hallucinogens, here are some steps to take:

◆ Create posters that warn about hallucinogens. Include telephone numbers of places people can call for help or for more information. Ask the owners or managers of places that kids and teens often go to if you can put up your posters. Try recreation centers, record stores, fast-food restaurants, pizza places, ice-cream parlors, candy stores, movie theaters, supermarkets, and youth centers.

◆ Write a letter about hallucinogens to the editor of the community and local newspapers.

◆ Create fact sheets about hallucinogens. Include telephone numbers of places that people can call for help or for more information. Ask local supermarkets if they will stuff your fact sheet in customers' bags.

◆ Ask local businesses, such as the gas or telephone company, to include bill stuffers about the dangers of hallucinogens.

Enjoy Drug-Free Fun

Looking good and feeling good are great reasons to avoid using hallucinogens and other drugs. Millions of young people across the United States stay free of hallucinogens and other harmful substances. They know that using drugs does not solve problems. Nor does it add anything to their lives.

There are lots of fun ways to enjoy life. For example, learning a new skill can be fun. How about learning a new language, taking dance lessons, or trying out for a play? Or take up skating, water or snow skiing, or skateboarding. Playing sports is another activity with plenty of choices: tennis, volleyball, soccer, basketball, baseball, hockey, or track, for example.

Writing stories or poetry can also be a lot of fun. There are magazines that publish young people's stories or poems. Creating greeting cards for a local gift or card shop can also be fun.

Volunteer work at a hospital, day care center, food bank, nature center, or nursing home can be very fulfilling. Volunteering to teach people to read or reading for people who cannot see are also rewarding.

Want to make some money? Baby-sitting, doing yard work, cleaning basements or attics, washing cars, or doing other odd jobs can help someone and earn money at the same time.

Linking up with a mentor is a great idea for many kids. Check with the school counselor about a mentoring program, or call the local Big Brother/Big Sister organization.

Peer support groups at schools can help kids discuss and deal with daily life issues and decisions, offer fun activities, and sometimes increase cultural awareness. Check into after-school youth programs or groups such as Boys and Girls Clubs of America, Cub Scouts, Boy Scouts, and Girl Scouts. You can also join or start a group that brings together kids who like to do photography, cook, camp, or learn about the wildlife in the area. Belonging to groups such as these is a great way to meet new friends and do exciting activities and projects.

Like to help others? Look into peer leadership programs and peer counseling interventions at school or the community center. These programs help young people learn how to speak before an audience, organize tasks, talk with peers and adults, and to run group meetings. Peer leaders sometimes speak at conferences and meetings or colead drug prevention activities. Peer

Millions of young people stay free of hallucinogens every day. Learning a new skill, such as inline skating can be a fun, healthy alternative to drug use.

counseling interventions involve young people who help their peers through one-on-one sessions, informal street talks, or answering a telephone hot line.

Here are some examples of what kids are doing as peer leaders and peer counselors:

◆ Each year in Kyle, South Dakota, selected students at Little Wound School are trained as peer counselors. They learn how to counsel groups and individuals. Peer counselors give presentations on drug abuse in their communities and school. They also carry out other projects to lower drug use.

◆ Young people in Atlanta, Georgia, can join a program called Super Stars. Super Star sessions are held in the early evening at a school or community center. There, young people learn about drug abuse and how to say no to drugs. They also develop decision-making skills and build their confidence with fun activities.

◆ Everyday Theater serves African-American preteens and teens in Washington, D.C. Each year, the program includes a summer theater for young people, an on-the-job training program for older teens, and an after-school program for all. Kids in Everyday Theater help develop an original play. They then perform the play in eighteen places throughout Washington, D.C. In this way, Everyday Theater reaches thousands of preteens and teens with information about drug abuse.

◆ Project Venture in New Mexico is held every year in four American Indian communities. It includes summer leadership camps and year-round programs and activities in schools and communities. Project Venture gives kids the chance to enjoy drug-free fun such as camping trips, rock climbing, rappelling, rope courses, and canoeing. In addition, older teens are trained to become big brothers and big sisters to younger kids. This project has the only fully certified search and rescue teams in the United States made up of all American Indian students.

questions for discussion

1. How many young people do you know who have or are using hallucinogens? How do you feel about their hallucinogen use?

2. What would you do if someone wanted you to try a hallucinogen?

3. Are hallucinogens talked about in your school's drug education classes? If not, do you think you will recommend that hallucinogens be included?

4. Have you talked to your parents about hallucinogens? Some parents know about other drugs such as alcohol and marijuana, but not about hallucinogens.

5. What do you like to do to get a natural high? Many kids like to swim, play basketball, baseball, soccer or tennis, skate, write, draw or paint, or do crafts.

6. What would be three or four things you would tell a friend who asked you about LSD or other hallucinogens?

7. What reasons not to try hallucinogens would you offer to a friend who wanted to try them?

8. Both PCP and ketamine deaden pain. How can this be dangerous for users?

9. Hallucinogens often have a variety of street names. Do you think this makes these drugs more enticing or interesting?

chapter notes

Chapter 1. Joe's Story

1. Al Sicherman, "A Father's Plea: Be Scared for Your Kids," *Johnson Institute Newsletter*, undated, p. 3.

2. Ibid.

3. Ibid., p. 6.

4. Ibid., p. 3.

Chapter 2. Society and Hallucinogens

1. Joseph B. Treaster, "Use of LSD, Drug of Allure and Risk, Is Said to Rise," *The New York Times*, December 27, 1991, p. 32.

2. "The Negative Side of Nostalgia: The Resurgence of LSD Drug Abuse," *Medical Update*, July 1993, pp. 3–5.

3. "Drug Use Among American Teens Shows Some Signs of Leveling After a Long Rise," The University of Michigan press release, December 18, 1997.

4. Ibid.

5. Author interview with "Bob," July 23, 1998.

6. Ibid.

7. "The Negative Side of Nostalgia: The Resurgence of LSD Drug Abuse," p. 3.

8. Ibid.

9. Treaster, p. 33.

10. Ibid.

11. Darryl S. Inaba, William E. Cohen, and Michael E. Holstein, *Uppers, Downers, All Arounders* (Ashland, Oreg.: CNS Publications, Inc., 1997), p. 224.

12. Center for Substance Abuse Prevention, *Hallucinogens: Tips for Teens* (Washington, D.C.: Substance Abuse and Mental Health Services Administration, U.S. Department of Health and Human Services, 1998), p. 1.

13. "The Negative Side of Nostalgia: The Resurgence of LSD Drug Abuse," p. 3.

14. Center for Substance Abuse Prevention, *Hallucinogens: Tips for Teens*, p. 1.

Chapter 3. Real-Life Stories

1. Author interview with "Bob," July 23, 1998.

2. "Missionary for Toad Venom Is Facing Charges," *The New York Times*, February 20, 1994, section 1, p. 19.

3. Leigh A. Henderson, and William J. Glass, eds. *LSD: Still with Us After All These Years* (New York: Lexington Books, An Imprint of Macmillan, Inc., 1994), pp. 18–19.

4. The American Council for Drug Education, *Flashback: Bad News for Bored Teens* (Rockville, Md.: The American Council for Drug Education, 1994), p. 19.

5. Henderson and Glass, p. 16.

6. Timothy Leary, *Flashbacks: An Autobiography*, (Los Angeles: J. P. Tarcher, Inc., 1983), p. 68.

7. Ibid., p. 118.

8. Ibid., p. 71.

9. Richard Jerome, and John Hannah, "Traveling Man," *People*, June 17, 1996, p. 176.

10. Ibid.

11. Trent Tschirgi, University of Maryland Office of Substance Abuse Studies, © 1996, <http://www.inform.umd.edu:8080/EdRes/Colleges/BSOS/Depts/Cesar/metnet/pcpc1.mnu> (November 1, 1996).

12. Ibid.

13. Don Colburn, "LSD: A Potent Trip," *Washington Post Health*, September 24, 1991, p. 19.

14. Ibid.

Chapter 4. Dangers of Hallucinogens

1. The American Council for Drug Education, *Flashback: Bad News for Bored Teens*, (Rockville, Md., The American Council for Drug Education, 1994), p. 19.

2. Ibid., p. 18.

3. Ibid.

4. Darryl S. Inaba, William E. Cohen, and Michael E. Holstein, *Uppers, Downers, All Arounders* (Ashland, Oreg.: CNS Publications, Inc., 1997), pp. 231–232.

5. Ibid., p. 232.

6. Trent Tschirgi, University of Maryland Office of Substance Abuse Studies, © 1996 http://www.inform.umd.edu:8080/EdRes/Colleges/BSOS/Depts/Cesar/metnet/pcpa3.mnu> (November 1, 1996).

7. Ibid.

8. Ibid.

9. Minnesota Prevention Resource Center, *Questions About Phencyclidine* (Anoka, Minn.: Minnesota Prevention Resource Center, 1990), n.p.

10. Ibid.

11. The National Clearinghouse for Alcohol and Drug Information, *Ketamine: A Fact Sheet* (Rockville, Md.: SAMHSA, 1997).

12. John Cloud, "Is Your Kid on K," *Time*, October 20, 1997, p. 91.

13. Inaba et al., p. 228.

14. Ibid.

15. Ibid., p. 180.

16. Author interview with "Bob," July 23, 1998.

Chapter 5. Fighting Drug Abuse

1. Andrew Mecca and James Kooler, "California's Mentoring Initiative," *Prevention Pipeline*, September/October 1997, p. 5.

2. "Elks' Prevention Efforts Span Nation," *ViewPoint*, Spring 1997, p. 10.

Chapter 6. What You Can Do

No notes.

glossary

acquired immunodeficiency syndrome (AIDS)—A deadly disorder of the immune system. It lowers the body's ability to fight off infectious bacteria and viruses.

black market—An illegal market or illegal selling and buying of products or services.

flashback—A recurrence of a drug-induced hallucinatory experience some time after the drug has been taken.

hallucinogen—A drug that if taken in small doses produces changes in perception, thought, and mood.

human immunodeficiency virus (HIV)—The virus that causes AIDS.

ketamine—A veterinary tranquilizer that is used by young people for its hallucinogenic effects. It is known on the street by many names, such as special k or vitamin k. Its effects are varied and unpredictable.

LSD (lysergic acid diethylamide)—A powerful hallucinogen discovered by experiments with the ergot fungus. It is now artificially made for sale on the black market.

magic mushrooms—Certain mushrooms that produce hallucinogenic effects.

mescal buttons—The hallucinogenic ingredient in the peyote plant.

microgram—One millionth of a gram.

PCP (phencyclidine)—A drug abused for its hallucinogenic effects. It is known on the street under many names, such as angel dust and rocket fuel. Its effects are varied and unpredictable.

peyote—A hallucinogenic cactus found in parts of Mexico and Texas. It is used among American Indians in religious ceremonies.

psilocin—A hallucinogenic ingredient found in magic mushrooms.

psilocybin—A hallucinogenic ingredient found in magic mushrooms.

psychoactive—Altering one's thinking, perceptions, and emotions. Drugs that do this are called psychoactive drugs.

side effects—Unwanted or negative effects from taking a drug.

synthetic—Artificially made from chemicals in a laboratory.

tolerance—Reduction of the response to a drug following its repeated use.

where to write

Alateen
P.O. Box 862
Midtown Station
New York, NY 10018–0862
(212) 302–7240
<http://www.alanon.com>

National Clearinghouse for Alcohol and Drug Information (NCADI)
P.O. Box 2345
Rockville, MD 20847–2345
1–800–729–6686
<http://www.health.org/index.htm>

National Families in Action (NFIA)
Century Plaza II
2957 Clairmont Road
Suite 150
Atlanta, GA 30329
(404) 248–9676
<http://www.emory.edu/NFIA/>

National Institutes on Drug Abuse and Alcohol Abuse
5600 Fishers Lane
Room 9A53
Rockville, MD 20857
(301) 443–1514
<http://www.nida.nih.gov/>

Partnership for a Drug-Free America
405 Lexington Avenue
16th Floor
New York, NY 10174
(212) 922–1560
<http://www.drugfreeamerica.org/>

further reading

Glass, George. *Drugs and Fitting In*. New York: Rosen Publishing Group, 1998.

Hyde, Margaret O. *Know About Drugs*. New York: Walker, 1996.

Littell, Mary Ann. *LSD*. Springfield, N.J.: Enslow Publishers, Inc. 1996.

Newman, Gerald, and Eleanor Newman Layfield. *PCP*. Springfield, N.J.: Enslow Publishers, Inc., 1997.

Phillips, Lynn. *Drug Abuse*. New York: M. Cavendish, 1994.

Robbins, Paul R. *Hallucinogens*. Springfield, N.J.: Enslow Publishers, Inc.,1996.

Ross-Flanigan, Nancy. *Peyote*. Springfield, N.J.: Enslow Publishers, Inc., 1997.

Smith, Sandra Lee. *Peyote and Magic Mushrooms*. New York: Rosen Publishing Group, 1995.

Substance Abuse and Mental Health Services Administration. *Tips for Teens: Hallucinogens*. Washington, D.C.: U.S. Department of Health and Human Services, n.d.

Internet Addresses

Indiana Prevention Resource Center
<http://www.drugs.indiana.edu/>

Join Together Online
<http://www.jointogether.org>

Wisconsin Clearinghouse, University of Wisconsin-Madison University Health Services
<http://www.uhs.wisc.edu/wch/>

index